The Love Song of J. Alfred Prufrock and Other Works

by T. S. Eliot

Includes MLA Style Citations for Scholarly Secondary Sources, Peer-Reviewed Journal Articles and Critical Essays

The Love Song of J. Alfred Prufrock and Other Works

by T. S. Eliot

A Squid Ink Classic

[Squid Ink Classics Edition]

November 2015

Boston, MA

CONTENTS

The Love Song of J. Alfred Prufrock

S'io credesse che mia risposta fosse

A persona che mai tornasse al mondo,

Questa fiamma staria senza piu scosse.

Ma perciocche giammai di questo fondo

Non torno vivo alcun, s'i'odo il vero,

Senza tema d'infamia ti rispondo.

Let us go then, you and I,

When the evening is spread out against the sky

Like a patient etherized upon a table;

Let us go, through certain half-deserted streets,

The muttering retreats

Of restless nights in one-night cheap hotels

And sawdust restaurants with oyster-shells:

Streets that follow like a tedious argument

Of insidious intent

To lead you to an overwhelming question ...

Oh, do not ask, "What is it?"

Let us go and make our visit.

In the room the women come and go

Talking of Michelangelo.

The yellow fog that rubs its back upon the window-panes,

The yellow smoke that rubs its muzzle on the window-panes,

Licked its tongue into the corners of the evening,

Lingered upon the pools that stand in drains,

Let fall upon its back the soot that falls from chimneys,

Slipped by the terrace, made a sudden leap,

And seeing that it was a soft October night,

Curled once about the house, and fell asleep.

And indeed there will be time

For the yellow smoke that slides along the street,

Rubbing its back upon the window-panes;

There will be time, there will be time

To prepare a face to meet the faces that you meet;

There will be time to murder and create,

And time for all the works and days of hands

That lift and drop a question on your plate;

Time for you and time for me,

And time yet for a hundred indecisions,

And for a hundred visions and revisions,

Before the taking of a toast and tea.

In the room the women come and go

Talking of Michelangelo.

And indeed there will be time

To wonder, "Do I dare?" and, "Do I dare?"

Time to turn back and descend the stair,

With a bald spot in the middle of my hair—

(They will say: "How his hair is growing thin!")

My morning coat, my collar mounting firmly to the chin,

My necktie rich and modest, but asserted by a simple pin—

(They will say: "But how his arms and legs are thin!")

Do I dare

Disturb the universe?

In a minute there is time

For decisions and revisions which a minute will reverse.

For I have known them all already, known them all:

Have known the evenings, mornings, afternoons,

I have measured out my life with coffee spoons;

I know the voices dying with a dying fall

Beneath the music from a farther room.

So how should I presume?

And I have known the eyes already, known them all—

The eyes that fix you in a formulated phrase,

And when I am formulated, sprawling on a pin,

When I am pinned and wriggling on the wall,

Then how should I begin

To spit out all the butt-ends of my days and ways?

And how should I presume?

And I have known the arms already, known them all—

Arms that are braceleted and white and bare

(But in the lamplight, downed with light brown hair!)

Is it perfume from a dress

That makes me so digress?

Arms that lie along a table, or wrap about a shawl.

And should I then presume?

And how should I begin?

*   *   *   *

Shall I say, I have gone at dusk through narrow streets

And watched the smoke that rises from the pipes

Of lonely men in shirt-sleeves, leaning out of windows?

...

I should have been a pair of ragged claws

Scuttling across the floors of silent seas.

*   *   *   *

And the afternoon, the evening, sleeps so peacefully!

Smoothed by long fingers,

Asleep ... tired ... or it malingers,

Stretched on the floor, here beside you and me.

Should I, after tea and cakes and ices,

Have the strength to force the moment to its crisis?

But though I have wept and fasted, wept and prayed,

Though I have seen my head (grown slightly bald) brought in upon a platter,

I am no prophet—and here's no great matter;

I have seen the moment of my greatness flicker,

And I have seen the eternal Footman hold my coat, and snicker,

And in short, I was afraid.

And would it have been worth it, after all,

After the cups, the marmalade, the tea,

Among the porcelain, among some talk of you and me,

Would it have been worth while,

To have bitten off the matter with a smile,

To have squeezed the universe into a ball

To roll it toward some overwhelming question,

To say: "I am Lazarus, come from the dead,

Come back to tell you all, I shall tell you all"—

If one, settling a pillow by her head,

Should say: "That is not what I meant at all;

That is not it, at all."

And would it have been worth it, after all,

Would it have been worth while,

After the sunsets and the dooryards and the sprinkled streets,

After the novels, after the teacups, after the skirts that trail along the

floor—

And this, and so much more?—

It is impossible to say just what I mean!

But as if a magic lantern threw the nerves in patterns on a screen:

Would it have been worth while

If one, settling a pillow or throwing off a shawl,

And turning toward the window, should say:

"That is not it at all,

That is not what I meant, at all."

* * * *

No! I am not Prince Hamlet, nor was meant to be;

Am an attendant lord, one that will do

To swell a progress, start a scene or two,

Advise the prince; no doubt, an easy tool,

Deferential, glad to be of use,

Politic, cautious, and meticulous;

Full of high sentence, but a bit obtuse;

At times, indeed, almost ridiculous—

Almost, at times, the Fool.

I grow old ... I grow old ...

I shall wear the bottoms of my trousers rolled.

Shall I part my hair behind? Do I dare to eat a peach?

I shall wear white flannel trousers, and walk upon the beach.

I have heard the mermaids singing, each to each.

I do not think that they will sing to me.

I have seen them riding seaward on the waves

Combing the white hair of the waves blown back

When the wind blows the water white and black.

We have lingered in the chambers of the sea

By sea-girls wreathed with seaweed red and brown

Till human voices wake us, and we drown.

Portrait of a Lady

> Thou hast committed—
>
> Fornication: but that was in another country,
>
> And besides, the wench is dead.
>
> The Jew Of Malta

I

Among the smoke and fog of a December afternoon
You have the scene arrange itself—as it will seem to do—

With "I have saved this afternoon for you";
And four wax candles in the darkened room,
Four rings of light upon the ceiling overhead,
An atmosphere of Juliet's tomb
Prepared for all the things to be said, or left unsaid.
We have been, let us say, to hear the latest Pole
Transmit the Preludes, through his hair and finger tips.
"So intimate, this Chopin, that I think his soul
Should be resurrected only among friends
Some two or three, who will not touch the bloom
That is rubbed and questioned in the concert room."

—And so the conversation slips

Among velleities and carefully caught regrets

Through attenuated tones of violins

Mingled with remote cornets

And begins.

"You do not know how much they mean to me, my friends,

And how, how rare and strange it is, to find

In a life composed so much, so much of odds and ends,

(For indeed I do not love it ... you knew? you are not blind!

How keen you are!)

To find a friend who has these qualities,

Who has, and gives

Those qualities upon which friendship lives.

How much it means that I say this to you—

Without these friendships—life, what cauchemar!"

Among the windings of the violins

And the ariettes

Of cracked cornets

Inside my brain a dull tom-tom begins

Absurdly hammering a prelude of its own,

Capricious monotone

That is at least one definite "false note."

—Let us take the air, in a tobacco trance,

Admire the monuments

Discuss the late events,

Correct our watches by the public clocks.

Then sit for half an hour and drink our bocks.

II

Now that lilacs are in bloom

She has a bowl of lilacs in her room

And twists one in her fingers while she talks.

"Ah, my friend, you do not know, you do not know

What life is, you who hold it in your hands";

(Slowly twisting the lilac stalks)

"You let it flow from you, you let it flow,

And youth is cruel, and has no remorse

And smiles at situations which it cannot see."

I smile, of course,

And go on drinking tea.

"Yet with these April sunsets, that somehow recall
My buried life, and Paris in the Spring,
I feel immeasurably at peace, and find the world
To be wonderful and youthful, after all."

The voice returns like the insistent out-of-tune
Of a broken violin on an August afternoon:
"I am always sure that you understand
My feelings, always sure that you feel,
Sure that across the gulf you reach your hand.

You are invulnerable, you have no Achilles' heel.
You will go on, and when you have prevailed
You can say: at this point many a one has failed.

But what have I, but what have I, my friend,
To give you, what can you receive from me?
Only the friendship and the sympathy
Of one about to reach her journey's end.

I shall sit here, serving tea to friends...."

I take my hat: how can I make a cowardly amends

For what she has said to me?

You will see me any morning in the park

Reading the comics and the sporting page.

Particularly I remark

An English countess goes upon the stage.

A Greek was murdered at a Polish dance,

Another bank defaulter has confessed.

I keep my countenance,

I remain self-possessed

Except when a street piano, mechanical and tired

Reiterates some worn-out common song

With the smell of hyacinths across the garden

Recalling things that other people have desired.

Are these ideas right or wrong?

III

The October night comes down; returning as before

Except for a slight sensation of being ill at ease

I mount the stairs and turn the handle of the door

And feel as if I had mounted on my hands and knees.

"And so you are going abroad; and when do you return?
But that's a useless question.
You hardly know when you are coming back,
You will find so much to learn."
My smile falls heavily among the bric-a-brac.

"Perhaps you can write to me."
My self-possession flares up for a second;
This is as I had reckoned.
"I have been wondering frequently of late
(But our beginnings never know our ends!)
Why we have not developed into friends."
I feel like one who smiles, and turning shall remark
Suddenly, his expression in a glass.
My self-possession gutters; we are really in the dark.

"For everybody said so, all our friends,
They all were sure our feelings would relate
So closely! I myself can hardly understand.

We must leave it now to fate.

You will write, at any rate.

Perhaps it is not too late,

I shall sit here, serving tea to friends."

And I must borrow every changing

find expression ... dance, dance

Like a dancing bear,

Cry like a parrot, chatter like an ape.

Let us take the air, in a tobacco trance—

Well! and what if she should die some afternoon,

Afternoon grey and smoky, evening yellow and rose;

Should die and leave me sitting pen in hand

With the smoke coming down above the housetops;

Doubtful, for quite a while

Not knowing what to feel or if I understand

Or whether wise or foolish, tardy or too soon ...

Would she not have the advantage, after all?

This music is successful with a "dying fall"

Now that we talk of dying—

And should I have the right to smile?

Preludes

I

The winter evening settles down

With smell of steaks in passageways.

Six o'clock.

The burnt-out ends of smoky days.

And now a gusty shower wraps

The grimy scraps

Of withered leaves about your feet

And newspapers from vacant lots;

The showers beat

On broken blinds and chimney-pots,

And at the corner of the street

A lonely cab-horse steams and stamps.

And then the lighting of the lamps.

II

The morning comes to consciousness

Of faint stale smells of beer

From the sawdust-trampled street

With all its muddy feet that press

To early coffee-stands.

With the other masquerades

That time resumes,

One thinks of all the hands

That are raising dingy shades

In a thousand furnished rooms.

III

You tossed a blanket from the bed,

You lay upon your back, and waited;

You dozed, and watched the night revealing

The thousand sordid images

Of which your soul was constituted;

They flickered against the ceiling.

And when all the world came back

And the light crept up between the shutters,

And you heard the sparrows in the gutters,

You had such a vision of the street

As the street hardly understands;

Sitting along the bed's edge, where

You curled the papers from your hair,

Or clasped the yellow soles of feet

In the palms of both soiled hands.

IV

His soul stretched tight across the skies

That fade behind a city block,

Or trampled by insistent feet

At four and five and six o'clock

And short square fingers stuffing pipes,

And evening newspapers, and eyes

Assured of certain certainties,

The conscience of a blackened street

Impatient to assume the world.

I am moved by fancies that are curled

Around these images, and cling:

The notion of some infinitely gentle

Infinitely suffering thing.

Wipe your hand across your mouth, and laugh;

The worlds revolve like ancient women

Gathering fuel in vacant lots.

Rhapsody on a Windy Night

Twelve o'clock.

Along the reaches of the street

Held in a lunar synthesis,

Whispering lunar incantations

Dissolve the floors of the memory

And all its clear relations,

Its divisions and precisions,

Every street lamp that I pass

Beats like a fatalistic drum,

And through the spaces of the dark

Midnight shakes the memory

As a madman shakes a dead geranium.

Half-past one,

The street lamp sputtered,

The street lamp muttered,

The street lamp said,

"Regard that woman

Who hesitates toward you in the light of the door

Which opens on her like a grin.

You see the border of her dress

Is torn and stained with sand,

And you see the corner of her eye

Twists like a crooked pin."

The memory throws up high and dry

A crowd of twisted things;

A twisted branch upon the beach

Eaten smooth, and polished

As if the world gave up

The secret of its skeleton,

Stiff and white.

A broken spring in a factory yard,

Rust that clings to the form that the strength has left

Hard and curled and ready to snap.

Half-past two,

The street lamp said,

"Remark the cat which flattens itself in the gutter,

Slips out its tongue

And devours a morsel of rancid butter."

So the hand of a child, automatic

Slipped out and pocketed a toy that was running along the quay.

I could see nothing behind that child's eye.

I have seen eyes in the street

Trying to peer through lighted shutters,

And a crab one afternoon in a pool,

An old crab with barnacles on his back,

Gripped the end of a stick which I held him.

Half-past three,

The lamp sputtered,

The lamp muttered in the dark.

The lamp hummed:

"Regard the moon,

La lune ne garde aucune rancune,

She winks a feeble eye,

She smiles into corners.

She smoothes the hair of the grass.

The moon has lost her memory.

A washed-out smallpox cracks her face,

Her hand twists a paper rose,

That smells of dust and old Cologne,

She is alone

With all the old nocturnal smells

That cross and cross across her brain.

The reminiscence comes

Of sunless dry geraniums

And dust in crevices,

Smells of chestnuts in the streets,

And female smells in shuttered rooms,

And cigarettes in corridors

And cocktail smells in bars."

The lamp said,

"Four o'clock,

Here is the number on the door.

Memory!

You have the key,

The little lamp spreads a ring on the stair,

Mount.

The bed is open; the tooth-brush hangs on the wall

Put your shoes at the door, sleep, prepare for life."

The last twist of the knife.

Morning at the Window

They are rattling breakfast plates in basement kitchens,

And along the trampled edges of the street

I am aware of the damp souls of housemaids

Sprouting despondently at area gates.

The brown waves of fog toss up to me

Twisted faces from the bottom of the street,

And tear from a passer-by with muddy skirts

An aimless smile that hovers in the air

And vanishes along the level of the roofs.

The Boston Evening Transcript

The readers of the Boston Evening Transcript

Sway in the blind like a field of ripe corn.

When evening quickens faintly in the street,

Wakening the appetites of life in some

And to others bringing the Boston Evening Transcript,

I mount the steps and ring the bell, turning

Wearily, as one would turn to nod good-bye to Rochefoucauld

If the street were time and he at the end of the street,

And I say, "Cousin Harriet, here is the Boston Evening Transcript."

Aunt Helen

Miss Helen Slingsby was my maiden aunt,

And lived in a small house near a fashionable square

Cared for by servants to the number of four.

Now when she died there was silence in heaven

And silence at her end of the street.

The shutters were drawn and the undertaker wiped his feet—

He was aware that this sort of thing had occurred before.

The dogs were handsomely provided for,

But shortly afterwards the parrot died too.

The Dresden clock continued ticking on the mantelpiece,

And the footman sat upon the dining-table

Holding the second housemaid on his knees—

Who had always been so careful while her mistress lived.

Cousin Nancy

Miss Nancy Ellicot

Strode across the hills and broke them

Rode across the hills and broke them—

The barren New England hills

Riding to hounds

Over the cow-pasture.

Miss Nancy Ellicott smoked

And danced all the modern dances;

And her aunts were not quite sure how they felt about it,

But they knew that it was modern.

Upon the glazen shelves kept watch

Matthew and Waldo, guardians of the faith,

The army of unalterable law.

Mr. Apollinax

When Mr. Apollinax visited the United States

His laughter tinkled among the teacups.

I thought of Fragilion, that shy figure among the birch-trees,

And of Priapus in the shrubbery

Gaping at the lady in the swing.

In the palace of Mrs. Phlaccus, at Professor Channing-Cheetah's

He laughed like an irresponsible foetus.

His laughter was submarine and profound

Like the old man of the seats

Hidden under coral islands

Where worried bodies of drowned men drift down in the green silence,

Dropping from fingers of surf.

I looked for the head of Mr. Apollinax rolling under a chair,

Or grinning over a screen

With seaweed in its hair.

I heard the beat of centaurs' hoofs over the hard turf

As his dry and passionate talk devoured the afternoon.

"He is a charming man"—"But after all what did he mean?"—

"He has pointed ears ... he must be unbalanced,"—

"There was something he said that I might have challenged."

Of dowager Mrs. Phlaccus, and Professor and Mrs. Cheetah

I remember a slice of lemon and a bitten macaroon.

Hysteria

As she laughed I was aware of becoming involved in her laughter and

being part of it, until her teeth were only accidental stars with a

talent for squad-drill. I was drawn in by short gasps, inhaled at

each momentary recovery, lost finally in the dark caverns of her

throat, bruised by the ripple of unseen muscles. An elderly waiter

with trembling hands was hurriedly spreading a pink and white checked

cloth over the rusty green iron table, saying: "If the lady and

gentleman wish to take their tea in the garden, if the lady and

gentleman wish to take their tea in the garden ..." I decided that

if the shaking of her breasts could be stopped, some of the fragments

of the afternoon might be collected, and I concentrated my attention

with careful subtlety to this end.

Conversation Galante

I observe: "Our sentimental friend the moon

Or possibly (fantastic, I confess)

It may be Prester John's balloon

Or an old battered lantern hung aloft

To light poor travellers to their distress."

She then: "How you digress!"

And I then: "Some one frames upon the keys

That exquisite nocturne, with which we explain

The night and moonshine; music which we seize

To body forth our own vacuity."

She then: "Does this refer to me?"

"Oh no, it is I who am inane."

"You, madam, are the eternal humorist

The eternal enemy of the absolute,

Giving our vagrant moods the slightest twist

With your air indifferent and imperious

At a stroke our mad poetics to confute—"

And—"Are we then so serious?"

La Figlia Che Piange

Stand on the highest pavement of the stair—

Lean on a garden urn—

Weave, weave the sunlight in your hair—

Clasp your flowers to you with a pained surprise—

Fling them to the ground and turn

With a fugitive resentment in your eyes:

But weave, weave the sunlight in your hair.

So I would have had him leave,

So I would have had her stand and grieve,

So he would have left

As the soul leaves the body torn and bruised

As the mind deserts the body it has used.

I should find

Some way incomparably light and deft,

Some way we both should understand,

Simple and faithless as a smile and shake of the hand.

She turned away, but with the autumn weather

Compelled my imagination many days,

Many days and many hours:

Her hair over her arms and her arms full of flowers.

And I wonder how they should have been together!

I should have lost a gesture and a pose.

Sometimes these cogitations still amaze

The troubled midnight and the noon's repose.

MLA Style Citations for Scholarly Secondary Sources, Peer-Reviewed Journal Articles and Critical Essays

Childs, Donald J. "Knowledge and Experience in the Love Song of J. Alfred Prufrock." ELH 55 (Fall 1988): 685-699. Print.

Donoghue, Denis. "Beginning." The Southern Review 34.3 (1998): 532+. Literature Resource Center. Web.

Fleissner, Robert F. "Reverberations of Prufrock's Evening Performance in Aiken's Morning Song of Senlin." CLA Journal 36.1 (Sept. 1992): 31-40. Rpt. in Poetry Criticism. Ed. Laura A. Wisner-Broyles. Vol. 26. Detroit: Gale, 1999. Poetry Criticism Online. Web.

Fryxell, Donald R. "Understanding the Love Song of J. Alfred Prufrock." Robert Frost's Chicken Feathers and Other Lectures. Ed. Arthur R. Husboe.
The Augustana College Press, 1969. 33-44. Rpt. in Poetry Criticism. Ed. Ellen McGeagh. Vol. 31. Detroit: Gale, 2001. Poetry Criticism Online. Web.

Griffiths, D. "Daring to disturb the universe: Heidegger's authenticity and The Love Song of J.
Alfred Prufrock/Die heelal durf versteur: outentisiteit by

Heidegger en in The love song of J.
Alfred Prufrock." Literator: Journal of Literary Criticism, Comparative Linguistics and Literary Studies 30.2 (2009): 107+. Literature Resource Center. Web.

Knapp, James F. "Eliot's Prufrock." and The Form of Modern Poetry, in The Arizona Quarterly 30.1 (Spring 1974): 5-14. Rpt. in Contemporary Literary Criticism. Ed. Carolyn Riley and Phyllis Carmel Mendelson. Vol. 6. Detroit: Gale, 1976. Contemporary Literary Criticism Online. Web.

Locke, Frederick W. "Dante and T. S.
Eliot's Prufrock." Modern Language Notes. Vol. 78. The John Hopkins Press, 1963. 51-59. Rpt. in Poetry Criticism. Ed. Ellen McGeagh. Vol. 31. Detroit: Gale, 2001. Poetry Criticism Online. Web.

Lowe, Peter. "Prufrock in St. Petersburg: the presence of Dostoyevsky's Crime and Punishment in T. S. Eliot's 'The Love Song of J. Alfred Prufrock'." Journal of Modern Literature 28.3 (2005): 1+. Literature Resource Center. Web.

Mayer, Nicholas B. "Catalyzing Prufrock." Journal of Modern Literature 34.3 (2011): 182+. Literature Resource Center. Web.

McCulloch, Andrew. "The use of allusion in the love song of J. Alfred Prufrock." The English Review 12.2 (2001): 27+. Literature Resource Center. Web.

McNamara, Robert. "Prufrock and the Problem of Literary Narcissism." Contemporary Literature 27 (Fall 1986): 356-377. Rpt. in Poetry Criticism. Ed. Ellen McGeagh. Vol. 31. Detroit: Gale, 2001. Poetry Criticism Online. Web.

Rand, Thomas. "Eliot's 'The Love Song of J. Alfred Prufrock' and Shakespeare's Prince Hal: an unnoticed parallel." Yeats Eliot Review 22.4 (2005): 19+. Literature Resource Center. Web.

Saunders, Judith P. "The Love Song of Satin-Legs Smith: Gwendolyn Brooks Revisits Prufrock's Hell." Papers on Language & Literature 36.1 (2000): 3. Literature Resource Center. Web.

Schneider, Elisabeth. "Prufrock and After: The Theme of Change." Publications of the Modern Language Association of American 87.5 (Oct. 1972): 1103-1108. Rpt. in Poetry Criticism. Ed. Ellen McGeagh. Vol. 31. Detroit: Gale, 2001. Poetry Criticism Online. Web.

Smith, Grover. "Prufrock As Key to Eliot's Poetry." Approaches to Teaching Eliot's Poetry and Plays. The Modern Language Association of America, 1988. 88-93. Rpt. in Contemporary Literary Criticism. Ed. Jeffrey W. Hunter and Deborah A. Schmitt. Vol. 113. Gale, 1999. Contemporary Literary Criticism Online. Web.

Sultan, Stanley. "Tradition and the Individual Talent in Prufrock." Journal of Modern Literature 12.1 (Mar. 1985): 77-90. Rpt. in Poetry Criticism. Ed. Ellen McGeagh. Vol. 31. Detroit: Gale, 2001. Poetry Criticism Online. Web.

Sultan, Stanley. "The Function of Prufrock for Criticism." T. S. Eliot Annual. Ed. Shyamal Bagchee. Vol. 1. The Macmillan Press Ltd, 1990. 155-196. Rpt. in Poetry Criticism. Ed. Ellen McGeagh. Vol. 31. Detroit: Gale, 2001. Poetry Criticism Online. Web.